DIVING AND SNORKELING GUIDE TO

Texas

Includes Inland, Coastal, and Offshore Sites

Barbara Dunn and Stephan Myers

Pisces Books ™
A division of Gulf Publishing Company
Houston, Texas

Publisher's note: At the time of publication of this book, all the information was determined to be as accurate as possible. However, when you use this guide, new construction may have changed land reference points, weather may have altered reef configurations, and some businesses may no longer be in operation. Your assistance in keeping future editions up-to-date will be greatly appreciated.

Also, please pay particular attention to the diver rating system in this book. Know your limits!

All photographs by Stephan Myers

Library of Congress Cataloging-in-Publication Data
Dunn, Barbara.
   Diving and snorkeling guide to Texas: includes inland, coastal, and offshore sites/Barbara Dunn and Stephan Myers.
      p. cm.
   "List of dive shops": p.
   ISBN 1-55992-032-7
   1. Diving, Submarine—Texas—Guide-books. 2. Skin diving—Texas—Guide-books. 3. Texas—Description and travel—1981—Guide-books. I. Myers, Stephan. II. Title.
GV840.S78D85 1990   89-48624
797.2′3′09764—dc20   CIP

Pisces Books
A division of Gulf Publishing Company
P.O. Box 2608, Houston, Texas 77252-2608

Pisces Books is a trademark of Gulf Publishing Company.

Printed in Hong Kong

10 9 8 7 6 5 4 3 2

Table of Contents

We hope you have a lot of "up-front and personal" encounters with the underwater critters of Texas—like this parrotfish in "far east" Texas (see page 44).

Introduction

When it comes to land and resources, there's just no place like Texas. The nearly 270,000 square miles that our state claims is so vast that it even encompasses the four major geographical areas found on the North American continent. We have our own Great Plains in north central Texas, Great Western High Plains in the Panhandle, Rocky Mountains in West Texas, and Gulf Coastal Plains along the coast. Within a day's drive, you can travel from endless sandy beaches to mile-high elevations in the Guadalupe Mountains, from the moist, heavy air of East Texas' piney woods to the parched desolation of the Panhandle.

There is one aspect about the land that is constant nearly all over the state and into the Gulf of Mexico. Beneath all this diversity, the immense forces of the Earth have formed faults hundreds of miles long. Some of these faults have trapped oil, while others have opened the surface to pulsing veins of ground water. The results of these changes can be seen in the crystalline, spring-fed lakes and rivers across the state. Offshore, similar forces changed the floor of the Gulf of Mexico, lifting isolated areas closer to the water surface, enabling tiny coral polyps to thrive and build immense coral reefs.

As you drive across the state to various dive sites, take some time to appreciate the stark contrasts in life and topography. Texas' diving is as diverse as its land and, because there's no place like Texas, that's saying a lot.

◀ *Marine organisms encrust every square inch of the underwater structures of a rig. A diver can see large barnacles, hydroids, bryzoans, and many colorful fish and interesting invertebrates.*

How To Use This Guide

Even if you own your own compressor and have a lake in your backyard, diving at any level of expertise requires a certain amount of preparation. This guide describes the most popular dive sites in Texas, and provides information necessary for planning safe and enjoyable dives.

The dive sites are grouped under three general diving areas: inland, coastal, and offshore. Read the introduction to the area you plan to dive. It describes particular diving requirements, safety tips, and other information that may not be included under your specific destination. At each site, information on location, closest air, and accommodations is given, along with specific diving facts such as water temperature, depth range, hazards, and current conditions.

Before embarking on a long-awaited dive trip, check out your gear and contact a dive shop near the site to get the latest diving and weather conditions (see pages 75–77). There is an equipment checklist on page 78 to make sure you don't forget anything important, and maps on pages 80–87 show parks and campgrounds near the various inland dive sites.

Definition of Ratings

Always rate your diving skills conservatively. Remember the adage that there are old divers and bold divers, but few old, bold divers. We consider a *novice diver* to be someone in decent physical condition who has recently completed a basic diving certification course, or is a certified diver who has not been diving recently, or who has no experience in similar waters. We consider an *intermediate diver* to be a certified diver in excellent physical condition who has been diving actively for at least a year following certification in a basic diving course, and who has been diving recently in similar waters. We consider an *advanced diver* to be someone who has completed an advanced certification diving course, or who has the equivalent experience, has been diving recently in similar waters, has been diving frequently for at least two years, and is in excellent physical condition.

The rating of a site is always based on normal water conditions. When water conditions change, so does your level of expertise. A serene river

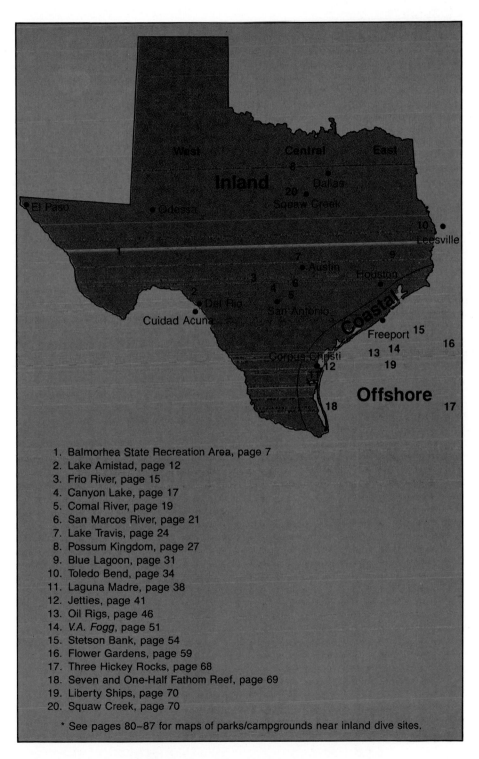

West   Central   East

Inland

8

El Paso   20   Dallas

Odessa   Squaw Creek

10

Leesville

7

Austin   9

3   Houston

2   4   6

Del Rio   5

Cuidad Acuna   San Antonio

Coastal

Freeport   15

13   14   16

Corpus Christi   19

12

Offshore

18   17

* See pages 80–87 for maps of parks/campgrounds near inland dive sites.

appropriate for novice divers can suddenly become a raging torrent after heavy rains. A quick call to a dive shop may save you time and money if conditions are hazardous.

Spearfishing Regulations

The Texas Department of Parks and Wildlife strictly regulates freshwater and saltwater fishing. Lakes and marinas are frequently patrolled, so be aware of the following rules:

▶ All spearfishing requires a fishing license. A saltwater stamp is necessary for coastal and offshore fishing.
▶ Spearfishing in most rivers is prohibited.
▶ It is unlawful to leave an edible or bait fish to die.
▶ Only non-game fish may be caught by speargun and spear. The following may **not** be spearfished:

Freshwater game fish: Blue catfish, brown trout, channel catfish, crappie (black and white), flathead catfish, Guadalupe bass, largemouth bass, red drum, rainbow trout, smallmouth bass, spotted bass, striped bass, walleye, white bass, and hybrids or subspecies of the above.

Saltwater game fish: Blue catfish, blue marlin, broadbill swordfish, brown trout, channel catfish, cobia, crappie (black and white), flathead catfish, Guadalupe bass, king mackerel, largemouth bass, red drum, rainbow trout, sailfish, smallmouth bass, snook, Spanish mackerel, spotted bass, spotted seatrout, striped bass, tarpon, wahoo, walleye, white bass, white marlin, and hybrids or subspecies of the above.

For further information, call the Texas Parks and Wildlife Department at 800-792-1112.

1

Inland Diving

If you look at a road map of Texas, you'll find a dense web of roadways and towns in east and central Texas. About a thumb's width left of San Antonio, it all evaporates, leaving a few wispy strands to stretch into the empty vastness of West Texas. The picture's basically the same for diving locations. Even though Texas has 5,024 square miles of inland waterways (second only to Alaska), most are in the eastern half of the state. Only three of the twenty sites in this guide lie west of San Antonio, but they are well worth the trip. The cleansing action of water moving through porous, underground rocks and shallow, fast-flowing rivers produces exceptional clarity.

The diversity of inland diving encompasses rivers, lakes, and springs. Without question, spring-fed rivers and lakes offer the finest water conditions. Balmorhea and the Frio, San Marcos, and Comal Rivers are perpetually filled with crystalline water at consistent 70° to 72°F temperatures. The lakes are actually reservoirs, pooling water from the "big" rivers—the Rio Grande, Colorado, Brazos, and Sabine. Although visibility in the lakes varies widely, their depth and diversity of plants and wildlife are big attractions. Most life can be found in the top 30 feet, although a few have deep sunken forests. Nearly all the lakes have sunken boats, cars, and other objects to explore.

Tips for Inland Diving

Wetsuits. We recommend wearing a full wetsuit or jumpsuit when drift-diving in rivers to avoid injury from rocks and branches. Most divers also wear wetsuits in spring-fed waters, especially when outside temperatures are 60°F or less.

Knives. As a general rule, carry a knife when diving in lakes so you can free yourself from any entanglements with vegetation or monofilament.

5

Although the Blue Lagoon caters primarily to scuba classes, it is also open for recreational diving (see page 31).

Crowds. Dive on a weekday, if at all possible. On weekends and holidays, most of the lakes and rivers attract large numbers of boats, waterskiers, jet skiers, tubers, and fishermen, and this has a marked effect on visibility. Tubers are pretty harmless and can provide some entertaining views from 10 feet below. Just remember to look up before you surface.

Hazards

Dams. Avoid them, especially the turbochannels and spillways.

Caves. There are a variety of caves, grottos, loops, and shoots in the lakes, especially along cliffs. Novices have no business going inside caves. They can be deathtraps even for the most experienced divers. This guide does not list places that don't have enough room for a diver to turn around.

Heavy rains. Rivers can become deep and fast-flowing after heavy rains. Unless you are an exceptionally strong swimmer, wait a few days until the water calms down.

Closest town/air:	Balmorhea/Odessa (100 miles)
Typical depth range:	7–25 feet
Typical water conditions/	
temperature:	Calm/72–76°F year round
Visibility:	40–80 feet
Expertise required:	Novice
Access:	Concrete walkway (see map on page 80)

Deep in the heart of West Texas, where heat turns highways into molten ribbons and the scrubby creosote bush of the Chihuahuan desert casts a mere few inches of shade, San Solomon Spring bubbles forth an amazing 26 million gallons of pure spring water every day. The spring erupts at Balmorhea State Recreation Area, an oasis set among the foothills of the Davis Mountains four miles west of Balmorhea on U.S. 290.

Here you'll find the best freshwater diving in Texas. A 1.75-acre pool, touted as the world's largest spring-fed swimming pool, was constructed

Balmorhea is the most misleading diving destination in Texas. Its surface appearance belies a wonderland of bubbling springs, numerous fish, and sparkling waters.

around the spring in 1935 by the Civilian Conservation Corps. The pool is designed in a 215-foot diameter circle over the spring. Concrete covers the first 4 to 7 feet around the pool, then moss-covered rocks slope down to a bottom depth of 30 feet. The bottom consists of rocks and a bubbling sandy area where the spring emerges.

Balmorhea may look like an ordinary swimming pool, but beneath the surface you'll discover that the extraordinary visibility and diverse wildlife rivals Florida's springs. Bring some morsels down and you'll be surrounded by Mexican tetras and catfish. But beware—the tetras nibble on *anything*.

You may see two endangered fish species, the Comanche Springs pupfish and the Pecos mosquitofish, along with minnows, perch, catfish, crayfish, and turtles.

Balmorhea offers a very controlled diving environment, which makes it a popular spot for open-water certification. Park officials regulate activities

Catfish and Mexican tetras abound in the pool's azure blue waters.

San Solomon Spring bubbles forth at several areas of the pool. The boiling sand attracts many small fish looking for food.

at the pool to accommodate both swimmers and divers. You may not dive in the nearby canals or in Lake Balmorhea. During winter hours (Labor Day through Memorial Day), the pool is open to only divers from 8:00 a.m. to sundown. Summer diving hours (Memorial Day through Labor Day) are 8:00 a.m. to 11:30 a.m. Every diver must have completed a dive class, review class or logged actual time in the water within the previous 18 months. Current certification cards and log books must be presented before signing a liability release. Absolutely no diver may dive alone.

Balmorhea is at least an 8-hour drive from Houston or Dallas, so plan your trip accordingly. Although the nearest air is 100 miles away in Odessa, dive classes are held frequently on summer weekends, so it may be possible to buy air on site. The park superintendent may be able to tell you whether a class is planned on the day of your dive.

Mexican tetras go into a feeding frenzy when divers and snorkelers bring down morsels of food.

Accommodations at the recreation area include camp sites, trailer hook-ups, bathing facilities, and an 18-room motel. A concession stand is open during the summer months. We suggest you call well in advance for reservations at the motel, and request current diving regulations before traveling to Balmorhea. *For more information,* contact the Park Superintendent, Balmorhea State Recreation Area, Box 15, Toyahvale, Texas 79786, or call (915) 375-2370.

Balmorhea appears larger than its actual size because of its visibility, which often exceeds 80 feet.

Closest city/air:	Del Rio/Lake Amistad
Winter/summer water temperature:	62°F/85°F
Typical depth range:	20–80 feet
Typical water conditions:	Slight current at edge of river channels
Visibility:	Averages 12 feet; can reach 35 feet from April to June
Expertise required:	Novice
Access:	Rocky hills, beaches, and boats (see map on page 81)

Covering 64,900 acres, this flood pool at the confluence of the Rio Grande, Pecos, and Devils Rivers is a joint project of the United States and Mexico. Amistad Dam, built in 1969, serves as a port of entry between the two countries. A line of buoys down the middle of the lake marks the international boundary line, and an opportunity for you honest folks out there who are a little short of funds. Drive a boat past the buoys, jump in

Although there are several access points at Lake Amistad, the limestone shore at Diablo East is the easiest and most popular.

Divers at Lake Amistad can explore rocky pinnacles, cliffs, and sunken objects, including two submerged ranch houses.

the water, take a deep breath, and . . . voila! You can now boast with the best about having been on an international dive trip.

Only one dive shop, Amistad Scuba Divers, serves the lake. Take Highway 90 West from Del Rio. The shop sits on the left side of the road about a mile *before* the bridge crossing the lake. About a mile from the dive shop is Diablo East, with a large, buoyed-off area with sunken boats, plenty of fish and grass at 12 feet. In spring, little freshwater jellyfish appear for a couple of weeks. Adjacent to the area are pinnacles with sharp drop-offs. Like wall dives, the pinnacles drop 150 feet into the old river channel. Also at Diablo East are the San Pedro Cliffs, a cove protected from boat traffic and exclusively for divers. Accessible by boat, it consists of cliffs, shear walls, and small fruit trees at 45 feet.

Lake Amistad's small fish seek protection among the lake grasses near the shore.

There are three good beach sites along the shore, and sunken cemeteries, railroad tracks, wrecks, and buildings to be explored. Other sites include an old sunken ranch house at Castle Canyon, Indian Springs in the Devils River arm, and the old sunken Highway 277 bridge running across San Pedro Canyon. On the Mexican side, there are fewer facilities, but diving is just as good and includes another sunken ranch up the Rio Grande arm.

Amistad offers some of the clearest lake diving in the state, partly because the reservoir is relatively new. Grass and tree decomposition have not yet affected water clarity, although visibility can decrease during hot, dry weather because of algae blooms. Call Amistad Scuba Divers for recorded diving conditions.

Numerous camping and boat rental facilities surround the lake. Del Rio is 12 miles downstream of the dam on U.S. 90, and the small, colorful town of Cuidad Acuna, Mexico, less than 10 miles west of Del Rio. Passports or automobile permits are not required to go into Cuidad Acuna. *For further information*, contact the National Park Service, Amistad Recreation Area at (512) 775-7491.

Closest city/air:	Uvalde
Winter/summer water temperature:	68°F/72°F
Typical depth range:	Shallow bed to 20 feet
Typical water conditions:	Generally mild, possible surge currents after heavy rains
Visibility:	10–20 feet
Expertise required:	Novice
Access:	Rocky, dirt banks (see map on page 82)

Frio means "cold" in Spanish, and you'll probably need a full wetsuit to dive here. Clear spring water feeds the Frio River from the Edwards Aquifer recharge zone. Most of the river is only 3–4 feet deep and lined with large, moss-covered rocks and boulders. The deeper, diveable portions of the river extend 20 miles along predominantly private property, so access is very limited.

Garner State Park, 31 miles north of Uvalde on U.S. 83, lies along a 1¹/₂ mile stretch of the river that has several pools ranging from 15 to 20 feet deep. Catfish, perch, bass, and carp are common here.

One of the few public access points for diving the Frio River is at Garner State Park. Below the spillway, several 15-foot depressions house schools of catfish, largemouth bass, and perch.

The crowds pack in to Garner on holidays and summer weekends, and tubers often float down from the spillway at the north end of the park. Plan to spend a few days to enjoy the scenery. The park is nestled in a scenic valley surrounded by high hills and cliffs that offer some spectacular panoramic views. Camping, showers and cabin rentals are available. *For more information*, contact the Park Superintendent, Garner State Park, Concan, Texas 78838, or call (512) 232-6132.

Numerous large boulders and a variety of aquatic plants decorate the cool, clear waters of the Frio.

Closest city/air:	New Braunfels/Canyon Lake
Winter/summer water temperature:	48°F/80°F
Typical depth range:	20–80 feet
Typical water conditions:	Calm
Visibility:	8–25 feet
Expertise required:	Novice
Access:	Rocky limestone shore (see map on page 83)

Canyon Lake lies 20 miles northeast of New Braunfels on FM 306. Steep-shouldered, evergreen hills surround this scenic 8,250-acre lake that abounds with largemouth bass, catfish, and blue gill perch. You'll probably need a wetsuit below the thermoclines, which sit at about 20 and 40 feet in the summer.

The most accessible dive spots are North Park, Comal Park, and Overlook Park. To reach North Park, turn left at the Chit Chat Lounge from FM 306.

The clearest near-shore water at Canyon Lake is at Overlook Park. The bottom plummets 100 feet from a short ledge into the old Guadalupe River channel.

The road leads to the edge of the lake, but you'll need to carry your gear about 50 yards. The silt and gravel bottom gradually slopes to three wrecked cars and a boat between 20 and 40 feet and a forest at 60 to 80 feet.

Comal Park is on the opposite side of the lake from North Park. Turn left on 2673 from FM 306 and go about 9 miles to Canyon Park Drive, turning right at the Circle-K gas station. Turn right again on Grandview, then left on Canyon Lake Forest. The entrance to Comal Park is the first right off Canyon Lake Forest. Here you can explore the ledges of the wall that drops to 90 feet about 20 feet from shore.

The best diving is at Overlook Park, across the dam from North Park. A steep hill leads to the shore. The bottom drops from 3 feet to 100 feet into the old Guadalupe river bottom, with treetops at 70 to 80 feet.

North Park has minimal camping facilities. Other lakeside accommodations can be found at Jacobs Creek, Canyon Lake, and Potters Creek Parks, or you may want to contact Deer Trail Lodge at (713) 935-2735 or Canyon Lake Cottages at (512) 964-3621.

A diver pauses at the end of a ledge at Overlook Park prior to descending a 100-foot limestone wall.

Comal River 5

Closest city/air:	New Braunfels
Typical depth range:	15 feet maximum
Typical water conditions:	72°F year round, minimal current, possible surge after heavy rains
Visibility:	5–25 feet
Expertise required:	Novice
Access:	Grassy and concrete embankments

Comal Springs feed the 4-mile long Comal River, which flows through the heart of New Braunfels. Like the San Marcos, the river's shallow depths make it a good snorkeling spot. The bottom consists of flat, white limerock slabs and silt with sparse vegetation. You'll see catfish, bass, perch, suckers, and the endangered freshwater prawn. Diving is divided into three areas—upper Comal, middle Comal and lower Comal.

The Comal River winds through the heart of New Braunfels, and provides a variety of recreational activities.

19

The most commonly seen fish in the Comal is the blue gill perch.

The upper Comal lies along Hinman Island at Landa Park. Landa Street will take you to the main entrance of the park. Turn right on Hinman Island Drive, which runs parallel to the river. Don't plan to dive the upper Comal on weekends. The gates to Hinman Island Drive are locked, and you'll have to carry your gear about 1/4 mile from the nearest parking area. Chances are you'll encounter more tubers than wildlife here.

Walk around the Tube Shoot and enter the water at the North Seguin Bridge to dive the middle Comal. It takes about an hour to dive this section. You can exit at the Coll Street Bridge, or continue on into the lower Comal.

The lower Comal provides the best diving. It is the longest and deepest part of the river and takes up to two hours to complete, even though on land it only extends the length of Coll Street. Stairs are available at the Coll Street Bridge and public parking is less than a block away. Make plans to have someone drive your car to the end of Coll Street at the exit. The end of this street is the *last* public exit. Get out here, or you'll take a freefall over a dam a little further downstream.

Tubers represent the worst and best aspects of diving the Comal. When they're out in large numbers, visibility can decrease to as little as five feet. They also tend to lose things in the water (like jewelry and money) and this makes the river a great place to treasure hunt.

The Gulf Coast Council of Diving Clubs hosts an annual "Trash Fest" at Hinman Island each October. Prizes are awarded to divers collecting the most trash from the river.

Accommodations are available in New Braunfels. Landa Park does not provide overnight camping.

San Marcos River 6

Closest city/air:	San Marcos
Typical depth range:	3–15 feet
Typical water conditions:	72°F year round, calm, possible surge currents after heavy rains
Visibility:	25 feet
Expertise required:	Novice
Access:	Concrete bank and sandy grass

Exceptional clarity and diverse wildlife make the San Marcos the best river dive in the state. More endangered species may live in the San Marcos River than any other freshwater body in Texas. The river begins at Spring Lake in Aquarena Springs, which is itself in the throes of a battle for survival. Continued drought in the Edwards Aquifer recharge zone and pumping of water by San Antonio for municipal uses is affecting water pressure at the springs. The clear, cool water we see here today may soon be altered, diminishing its beauty and abundance of wildlife.

The cool, clear water and abundant aquatic life of the San Marcos River attract divers, snorkelers, and underwater photographers.

Rare and endangered species find refuge in the beautiful San Marcos. The giant freshwater prawn, which can measure 20 inches long, usually hides during the day, but can easily be seen at night.

The best diving is accessed just beyond the spillway from Spring Lake in front of Pepper's Restaurant, and proceeds for 3/4 mile to Rio Vista Park at I.H. 35. Some people prefer to enter the water from the concrete banks at Sewall Park, a short distance downstream from Pepper's. Water depth ranges from only 3 to 8 feet up to Rio Vista Park, so you can enjoy the scenery equally well by just snorkeling. The water deepens to 15 feet at Rio Vista Park.

The San Marcos River teems with life. Forty different varieties of freshwater plants cover the bottom, including the rare and endangered Texas wild rice, found only in the San Marcos. You'll also see bass, giant mollies, Rio Grande and blue gill perch, catfish, turtles, Mexican tetras, and even the famous snail darter. Renegade goldfish appear once or twice a year, when semesters end at Southwest Texas State University.

Night dives bring out freshwater eels, red crawfish, and another endangered species, the giant freshwater prawn, which measures up to 20 inches in length. In the past, some folks have caught the freshwater prawn to take home for dinner. This is illegal and carries stiff penalties.

Diving in Aquarena Springs is allowed, but only on a *highly* restricted basis. Only advanced divers who have received an environmental impact briefing and are accompanied by a guide are permitted. Call Aquarena Springs Hotel at (512) 396-8900 for more information.

Texas wild rice can be viewed in several shallow areas of the river. This plant, found nowhere else in the world, is on the verge of extinction, and its existence is directly tied to the well-being of the river.

Closest city/air:	Austin/Lake Travis
Winter/summer water temperature:	60°F/85°F
Typical depth range:	20–70 feet
Typical water conditions:	Calm to slightly choppy
Visibility:	10–25 feet
Expertise required:	Novice
Access:	Rocky shore or boat (see map on page 84)

Lake Travis is one of the Highland lakes that stair-step up the Colorado River just outside of Austin. Someone caught a 200-pound catfish here a year ago, or so the story goes. Believe it or not, catfish "the size of a man or even a small car" do live in the 150-foot plus depths of the old river channel. Whiskered friends aside, Lake Travis is tremendously

Hill country scenery and diversity of dive sites make Lake Travis the most frequently dived lake in the state.

Some access points consist of steep rock ledges, so many divers prefer to gear up in the water.

popular for a few other reasons, like its beautiful setting among rolling hills, bikini-clad coeds from the University of Texas, romantic midnight sails, and impressive lakefront properties. On top of all this are its numerous and varied dive sites.

The easiest access is from Windy Point Park. Take Highway 183 north from Austin and turn west (left) on Loop 620. After crossing Mansfield Dam, take a right on Comanche Trail Road from 620 to Windy Point Road. Open year round (except Thanksgiving Day and Christmas Day), Windy Point Park offers carts to roll dive gear up to the lake's edge, an underwater guide to Windy Point, and concreted steps down to the water. The dive area is buoyed off 200 feet out into the water. From 30 feet down, you'll see a number of wrecked boats, cars, and other objects. A series of drop-offs extends down to a sunken forest of pecan trees from 90 to 110 feet.

Other sites are best accessed by boat. The northwest side of Starnes Island gradually slopes to 100 feet, with sunken boats at 25 and 60 feet. The area is buoyed off and has an underwater platform for dive classes. For more experienced divers, the other side of the island has good wall diving. The Walls at Marshall Ford Park drop in 50-foot increments into some of the deepest and clearest water in the lake. An interesting dive

Silt-covered boulders line the sides and bottom of Lake Travis, along with occasional submerged forests. Commonly seen fish are blue gill perch, Rio Grande perch, catfish, and buffalo carp.

between Hippy Hollow and Marshall Ford Park is the old shaker plant from the construction of the dam. Diving here extends to 110 feet and you'll see concrete pillars and pads and truck remnants. Night dives at Hippy Hollow include feeding white and black bass.

We recommend wearing a wetsuit below 60 feet during the summer. Beware of boaters and jet skiers on weekends and holidays, especially outside the buoys of Windy Point Park. Minimal camping is available at Windy Point Park and the Lower Colorado River Authority (LCRA) park near Mansfield Dam, with additional accommodations in Austin. *For further information*, contact Windy Point Park at (512) 266-9459 or a local dive shop (see page 75).

Closest city/air:	Caddo/Lake Possum Kingdom
Winter/summer water temperature:	55°F/82°F
Typical depth range:	10–85 feet
Typical water conditions:	Calm
Visibility:	5–10 feet
Expertise required:	Novice
Access:	Concrete, sandy beach, and boat (see map on page 85)

Lake Possum Kingdom covers 20,000 acres amid mesquite and junipers in the rocky canyons of the Palo Pinto Mountains. It was created with the construction of the Morris Sheppard Dam on the Brazos River in the late 1940s, and numerous quiet coves dot its 310-mile shoreline. Even before you see a road sign, you'll know this has got to be a "possum somewhere" because of the unbelievable numbers of possums.

Lake Possum Kingdom was created in the late 1940s with the construction of the Morris Sheppard Dam. Shore diving is generally done near Scuba Point, the only dive shop on the lake.

Divers can explore numerous sunken objects near shore as well as a variety of natural formations in deeper water.

Only one full service dive shop, Scuba Point, sits on the lake. It has a ramp, three pier docks, and a large area (250 × 300 feet) buoyed off in front of the shop. It boasts the world's largest dive-shop compressor, nicknamed "goldfinger," which was previously used in a commercial oxygen plant. The buoyed area in front has a gently sloping bottom with a variety of sunken objects for spatial reference. Be very careful of boat traffic when surfacing near the pier docks.

Boat access to other dive sites can be arranged through the dive shop. The Walls are cliffs that extend 80 to 100 feet into the water. Here you can explore along rock ledges and watch catfish and striped bass. The Cove is full of trees and grass with a flat bottom to about 50 feet, then a drop-off to 80 feet. A ledge at 70 feet forms a large cavelike area that extends under the cliff about 30 feet into pitch black darkness. Only experienced divers should go under the ledge.

Scuba Point provides free camping facilities. Cabins and a grocery store are available at Possum Kingdom Recreation Area located 45 miles away on the other side of the lake. *For more information,* call the dive shop at (817) 779-2482 or the Recreation Area at (817) 549-1803.

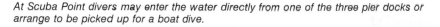

At Scuba Point divers may enter the water directly from one of the three pier docks or arrange to be picked up for a boat dive.

*Located near Huntsville, the Blue Lagoon consists of two flooded quartzite quarries.
The water's low pH discourages algal growth, contributing to visibility exceeding 50 feet.*

Closest city/air:	Huntsville/Blue Lagoon
Winter/summer water temperature:	60°F/90°F
Typical depth range:	15–35 feet
Typical water conditions:	Calm
Visibility:	15–60 feet
Expertise required:	Novice
Access:	Sandy beach and rocks (see map on page 86)

You may have heard of Texas' own "Cozumel in the Pines." This privately owned 100-acre site lies 6 miles northeast of Huntsville (70 miles north of Houston) among the towering pines of the Sam Houston National Forest. It was opened in 1986 as an open water training facility for scuba divers. The Blue Lagoon consists of two quartzite quarries, each about 6 acres, fed by artesian springs. The clear, Caribbean-like blue water provides visibility second only to Balmorhea in West Texas. Its low pH discourages

Both lagoons contain sunken boats. One of the highlights of diving in Lagoon I is exploring the 40-foot Chris Craft.

Alternating silty areas and rocky outcroppings form the bottom terrain of both lagoons.

growth of bacteria and vegetation. The only visible species is the dragonfly nymph, which looks and acts like a shrimp.

The Blue Lagoon offers the best easy dive in Texas and attracts more than 15,000 visitors annually. It's the perfect spot to fine-tune diving skills, practice underwater photography, and check out equipment. Maximum depth is 35 feet. To preserve visibility, 7 underwater platforms were constructed at about 30 feet to reduce disturbing the silty bottom during dive classes. The platforms also enable dive instructors to congregate with students and see the whole group at one time.

The east side of Lagoon I has beautiful, jagged cliffs that extend 20 feet below the water surface. Divers can see boulders the size of cars. Three

Weekend visitors find the Blue Lagoon an excellent place to enjoy night diving.

large sunken boats provide spatial reference and places to explore. Every Halloween the boats are converted into "haunted boats" with hidden skeletons, pumpkins, and sharks.

The Blue Lagoon caters only to divers. Swimming is allowed only for guests of divers and boating is prohibited. Accommodations include on-site camping, air, and bagged ice. Meals and additional accommodations are just 15 minutes away in Huntsville. The Blue Lagoon is open 7 days a week from mid-May through September (this can vary) and on weekends during other months. Daily admission charges are $10.00 for divers and $5.00 for nondivers. *For directions and additional information,* call the Blue Lagoon at (409) 291-6111.

Closest city/air:	Leesville, Louisiana (20 miles)
Winter/summer water	
temperature:	50°F/82°F
Typical depth range:	25–60 feet
Visibility:	10 feet
Expertise required:	Novice
Access:	Sandy (see map on page 87)

Ask someone on the east side of Toledo Bend where the Cajun gators are and he'll say, "De otre side." Ask someone on the west side of Toledo Bend where the Texas-size gators are and he'll say, "T'othur side." No one claims them, and few have actually seen them, but they're here.

Toledo Bend Reservoir is on the Sabine River on the Texas-Louisiana border. The water is clear, but tea-colored from leaf decomposition, and packed with fish and vegetation. A 15-to-20-foot-wide strip of grass grows 20 feet from the shore. The bottom is sandy silt covered with logs and

On-site parking and terraces make the north side of the dam the best access point at Toledo Bend.

limbs. You'll find red crawfish, freshwater clams, catfish, bass, and perch. Because of the vegetation and number of fishermen here, it is essential that you dive with a knife.

The best access and facilities are on the Louisiana side. From Burkville, Texas, take 692 north for 14 miles to Coffer Dam. The water is buoyed off about 20 feet away from a parking area at the end of the dam. A checkout platform, sunken cars, and other objects are within the buoys. Divers should avoid the floodgates that are a short distance north of the dive area.

Numerous islands are accessible by boat and generally have clearer water than along the shore. Most of the property on the Texas side is privately owned, but can be dived by boat. This water is deeper and has underwater cliffs about 100 yards from shore.

Camping is available at numerous lakeside locations in Louisiana. Toledo Bend lies on the outskirts of the Big Thicket, and the heat and humidity can be uncomfortable in summer. You may want to look into other accommodations in Leesville. *For further information,* contact the Sabine Parish Tourist and Recreation Commission in Many, Louisiana at (318) 256-5880.

Tannic acid from plant decomposition gives the water at Toledo Bend its unique coloration. A variety of grasses, some 15 feet tall, can be explored adjacent to the dam.

2

Coastal Diving

The coastline of Texas extends 624 miles from Louisiana to Mexico. Practically all of it is sandy beach, which is great for beachcombers, but unfortunately leaves few decent diving areas. The nearshore waters of the Gulf of Mexico carry a large amount of sediment in suspension, making visibility a couple of feet at most. If you swim out from shore to avoid breaking waves, you run into an area of unpredictable rip tides and undertows. We have chosen two sites that are comparatively safe, have decent visibility, and interesting marine life.

A snorkeler at the Laguna Madre. ▶

Closest city/air:	Corpus Christi
Winter/summer water temperature:	65°F/85°F
Typical depth range:	4–6 feet
Typical water conditions:	Calm
Visibility:	8–30 feet
Access:	Sandy beach

Beginning at Corpus Christi and running 113 miles south to Port Isabel, the Laguna Madre separates Padre Island, the longest barrier island in the United States, from the Texas mainland. The first 80 miles of Padre Island comprise the Padre Island National Seashore, an area of magnificent sand dunes, grasslands, and protected beaches. The best snorkeling spot at the

The shallow and grassy Laguna Madre offers spectacular snorkeling, especially in spring, before higher temperatures create plankton blooms.

Shallow water and brisk winds bring out windsurfers during summer months. Snorkelers should exercise extreme caution and frequently scan the horizon for nearby windsurfers.

Laguna is Bird Island Basin, a couple of miles from the National Seashore entrance on Park Road 22. It's also an excellent place to introduce potential divers into a safe and secure water environment.

The hard-packed beach at Bird Island Basin turns to marshmallow consistency in the water. About a hundred yards from shore, the sand disappears under dense beds of shoal grass. In July or August, you might see thousands of bay scallops buried in the sand. The grass beds are areas of very high biologic activity and provide a spawning ground for fish, clams and snails. Occasionally, you'll see a stingray or moon jelly, but the most prevalent residents are blue crabs, flounder, toadfish, redfish, mullet, speckled trout, and sponges.

The best time to snorkel is April to June, when the water is cooler and clearer. The Laguna water is extremely saline because of the depth (only two to three feet before the shoal grass beds) and the high rate of evaporation. It's a good idea to bring some fresh water to rinse off yourself and your equipment. Also, beware of windsurfers and light boats. The calm, shallow conditions that make the Laguna popular for snorkeling have also made it one of the top spots in the nation for windsurfing. They are very fast and virtually soundless. Try to snorkel during the week or early in the morning on weekends.

Accommodations are available in Corpus Christi and on Padre Island. Naturally, the closer you get to the water, the more expensive they become. Camping is allowed on the beach at Bird Island Basin.

Another campground with restrooms and showers is available 1/2 mile north of the Malaquite Visitor Center, a short distance south from Bird Island Basin on Park Road 22. Entrance to the National Seashore costs $3, and camping at Malaquite Beach is $4 per night. *For more information*, contact the Padre Island National Seashore Visitors Center at (512) 949-8069.

From May through August, the Laguna Madre serves as a spawning ground for a variety of fish and crustaceans. In some years, fascinating blue-eyed scallops cover vast areas of the Laguna bottom.

Closest city/air:	Aransas Pass
Winter/summer water temperature:	65°F/85°F
Typical depth range:	10–30 feet
Current conditions:	Variable; can be very strong
Visibility:	3–20 feet
Expertise required:	Intermediate
Access:	Rocks

The jetties extend Gulfward from Port Aransas at the northern tip of Mustang Island. Take the ferry from S.H. 136 across Aransas Pass to Port Aransas, or Park Road 53 from Padre Island. Parking is available on the beach at the south jetty, and a jetty ferry leaves every 1/2 hour to the north jetty.

Rocks located beneath the low tide line are thickly covered with marine algaes. It is advisable for buddies to help each other gear up while on these slippery rocks.

The marine algaes attached to the rocks resemble plants and grow in myriad forms and colors.

The jetties are rocky mounds 1/2 mile apart and one mile long, with the last 1/4 mile under water. The rocky rubble extends down about 20 feet to a sandy bottom. Visibility peaks from late summer to early fall, and is best on a daily basis between 10:00 a.m. and 2:00 p.m., when the sun is at its highest angle.

Algae, barnacles, sea urchins, and encrusting sponges cover the rocks, and the water is full of marine tropicals. Seeing octopus, barracuda, and sharks is not unusual, and spearfishing is popular. If you're interested in diving away from the jetties, you can follow one of the three lateral spurs that extend under water about 100 yards into the channel.

There are numerous hazards that divers should be aware of when diving the jetties: (1) Fishermen line the south jetty at 2-foot intervals on weekends. Use a dive flag and a knife, or go over to the north jetty where there are fewer crowds; (2) The currents here are unpredictable and can be very strong during tide changes; (3) Wear gloves and wetsuit (or some other cover) to protect against the barnacle-encrusted rocks. Passing water traffic creates waves that can throw you around; (4) Be careful of boat traffic on days of low visibility when diving near the channel; (5) Lastly, this is the site of the annual Texas Shark Fishing Contest. These aren't shark-infested waters, but if you're planning a night dive, remember their presence.

There is a wide selection of accommodations and dive shops in Port Aransas and Corpus Christi.

Most diving and snorkeling at the Aransas Pass jetties occurs close to the island. The waters are more protected here and there are usually fewer fishermen.

3

Offshore Diving

The Gulf of Mexico presents a unique diving environment. In other areas of the world, most open ocean diving consists of atolls and barrier reefs situated within a reasonable proximity to land. Gulf dive sites lie in deep water up to 120 miles from shore, where divers are subjected to the full force of currents and unpredictable weather. This is truly "open" ocean diving. Only divers with intermediate-level expertise or more should dive in these waters.

If you've never dived offshore, the shear numbers and diversity of wildlife will astound you. The flat and featureless floor of the Gulf makes any type of underwater structure a mecca for marine life seeking shelter and food. Whether natural or artificial, the dive sites display beautiful and fascinating communities of interdependent life.

On a conservation note, corals should be treated with care and respect. Coral polyps are soft and exposed, with little or no defense against poking or finning. Damaged polyps release symbiotic zoozanthellae (algae) out of their bodies and eventually die. One diver hurting one little polyp is not a tragedy, but hundreds of divers hurting hundreds of polyps is. Another adage: "Take only memories and leave only bubbles."

Warm water and calmer weather make summer and early fall the best seasons to dive offshore. Visibility is generally good close to shore, but can vary with the movement of plankton and sediment by nearshore currents. It can reach 125 feet at the Flower Gardens near the edge of the outer continental shelf. We strongly recommend that you make reservations a few months in advance of your planned trip. Some dive boats have all their weekends booked by the beginning of the dive season. Most reservations are arranged through dive shops, with those located near the coast having the best access to dive boats and offshore diving information.

Tips for Offshore Diving

Preparation: Make sure all your gear checks out before getting on the boat. Pack some medication if you're prone to seasickness. There's nothing like rolling on the seas for a few hours between dives.

Many offshore destinations are more than forty miles from shore. Larger vessels, specifically rigged for diving, are usually required to make these trips safe and enjoyable.

Entry/Exit: As a general rule, you should descend against the current and ascend with the current. You have more air and more energy at the beginning of a dive. Some sites are 50 feet or more below the surface, so follow the anchor line descending and ascending. A safety decompression stop should be made at ten feet before exiting the water.

Wetsuits: These should be worn on all offshore dives, especially at oil rigs.

Spearfishing: Carefully monitor your air supply, depth and nitrogen status, and don't shoot a fish with less than 1,500 psi in your tank. Because of the size of some of the fish offshore, we recommend adding a shock line to the cable. Dive shops usually sell and install a variety of spearfishing equipment.

Hazards

Orientation: *Never* go under water without a spatial reference point. Descend along rig legs or follow an anchor line all the way down to the site. Maintain a reference point throughout your dive. It doesn't take long at 70 feet to drift a few hundred yards from the dive boat.

Currents: There are some real "rip snorters" in the Gulf. They're not seasonal or predictable and can run to 4 knots.

Nearest point of departure:	Galveston, Freeport, Corpus Christi
Winter/summer water temperature:	65°F/84°F
Typical depth range:	Varies with distance from shore; can exceed 80 feet
Typical water conditions:	Highly variable
Visibility:	Varies with distance from shore; to 100 feet
Expertise required:	Intermediate

Offshore oil platforms are the most abundant form of reef community in the Gulf of Mexico. Hundreds of rigs dot the continental shelf off Texas and Louisiana. The underwater structures of a rig in 100 feet of water typically add 2 acres of hard surface to the water column.

If you're into marine biology, a rig is a fascinating place to explore a vertical marine community. Every square inch is covered by barnacles,

Large schools of Atlantic spadefish frequently investigate divers exploring the rig structures.

Hundreds of oil rigs dot the Texas coast, extending to the outer continental shelf. Each of these artificial reefs is like an underwater skyscraper or vertical zoo of marine life.

Divers can hand feed many reef denizens. Soap fish and damsel fish are easily lured by any type of table scrap.

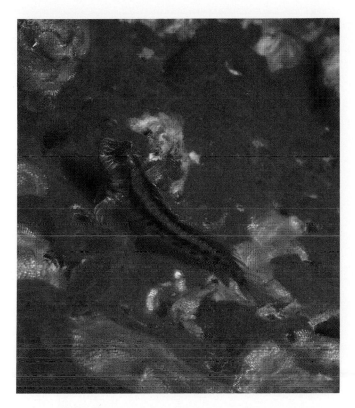

Numerous small blennies make their homes inside vacant barnacles. They are curious and, if approached slowly, can be viewed at close range.

encrusting sponges, bryzoans, and the occasional white hydroid or ivory bush coral. You can observe thousands of plate-sized spadefish schooling near the surface or flounder sifting through the muddy bottom. Soapfish, damselfish, blennies, butterflyfish, and angelfish dart through the maze of pipes and valves, avoiding the predatory jaws of barracuda, large amberjacks, and groupers.

Rig diving is considered to be the safest type of diving in the Gulf because depth can be controlled. You can dive at 5 feet or 150 feet, depending on how long you want your dive to last. However, you can expect to share a rig with some fishermen. Dive boat captains put up dive flags, and if you stay within the rig structure you're pretty well protected. Exercise some caution when surfacing inside the rig because wave action can throw you against the large, sharp barnacles that cover the rig legs.

The size of a rig can only be appreciated from under water. The legs of these artificial reefs can extend beyond the 200-foot range, and provide the option of multi-level diving.

These are excellent spearfishing sites. Before leaving shore, consult a dive shop for rigging your gun with stainless steel cable (barnacles can sever nylon) and a shock line. Also, don't shoot toward rig structures because they can deflect the spear toward other divers. *For more information*, contact a coastal dive shop (see page 77).

Nearest point of departure:	Freeport
Winter/summer water temperature:	65°F/84°F
Typical depth range:	65–100 feet
Typical water conditions:	Highly variable
Visibility:	30–80 feet
Expertise required:	Intermediate

Even for divers who frequently visit the *V.A. Fogg*, this wreck evokes a sense of awe and curiosity over its size and the tragedy that caused such staggering damage and loss of life. The *SS V.A. Fogg* disappeared 33 miles southeast of Freeport on February 1, 1972. The tanker was on its way to Galveston after unloading highly flammable benzene at Freeport. Three hours after its departure from Freeport, an explosion ripped through the

The wreck of the V.A. Fogg exudes an eerie and mysterious aura that intrigues divers.

The V.A. Fogg is a popular fishing spot. A diver examines tangled monofilament around a valve system encrusted with sponges.

Algae covers a massive anchor chain lying on the bow.

Undulating clouds of baitfish scurry in a single flash of silver at the slightest threat.

hull, killing all 39 crewmen and sinking the 572-foot, 12,500-gross ton tanker in less than two minutes. When the wreckage was located twelve days later, divers found pieces of steel plating 300 feet from the ship, massive internal damage, and blast marks from mid-ship forward. The condition of the tanker precluded any salvage operations, so the Coast Guard blasted the superstructure to 65 feet to prevent navigation hazards.

Today, the *V.A. Fogg* is a highly successful, unplanned artificial reef. She sits in 100 feet of water and is so large that at 80 feet, a diver will only see about one-tenth of the wreck. A carpet of green, brown, and red encrusting algae cover her hull, and clusters of hydroids, soft corals and stony, ivory bush coral dot the surface. Horned triggerfish, Atlantic spadefish, sergeant-majors, and angelfish roam around, and thousands of baitfish travel in undulating clouds. Commercial fishermen frequent the site for red snapper and bonita, but have to move when dive flags are up.

The ship's interior is dominated by encrusting sponges. We recommend advanced diving skills for interior diving because of the depth and lack of light. Although most divers don't spend much time inside the hull, you should be reasonably safe using a dive light and a safety line.

Nearest point of departure:	Freeport
Winter/summer water temperature:	65°F/84°F
Typical depth range:	60–90 feet
Typical water conditions:	Highly variable
Visibility:	30–110 feet
Expertise required:	Intermediate

Stetson Bank offers the most exhilarating dive on the Gulf Coast. Lying atop a salt dome 70.5 nautical miles southeast of Freeport in 180 feet of water, the vertically dipping claystones and siltstones form an outline resembling a Stetson hat, hence its name.

Stetson Bank is frequently described as looking like the surface of the moon. The upper reef area consists of large siltstones and claystones overlain by fire coral and encrusting sponges.

Abundant and diverse fish life attract divers to this marginal reef.

An underwater photographer pauses to shoot a 9-inch jackknife fish.

The well camouflaged scorpionfish is one of the few real hazards in the sea. Its dorsal spines are poisonous and can cause infection and great pain.

The white-spotted filefish roams the reef, feeding on sponges and fire coral.

A standard remark by first-time divers is, "Wow! I can't believe the number of fish down there!" For a marginal reef, Stetson has an amazingly diverse population of marine life. Covered in encrusting sponges and fire coral, the pinnacled surface at 60 to 90 feet swarms with schools of tropical fish and big game fish such as barracuda, amberjacks, and groupers. You'll stand a good chance of seeing sharks and giant stingrays. Even whale sharks occasionally visit.

A shy, golden-tailed moray peers out from among fire coral and encrusting sponges.

In a world of blue, the black dots and blue lines on the scrawled filefish help it blend into its environment.

If your dive boat anchors near the edge of the bank, you can set yourself up for a fascinating experience. Take some time to explore the crest, then drift out past the lip and over the edge. The inky black abyss that surrounds the bank seems to pull you down and conjures up some hair-raising and imaginative thoughts. Most divers explore along the walls over the edge, but some like to go out a few feet for a wider view. Keep your distance to a minimum and always maintain eye contact with the bank.

For you hardy souls who want to try a night dive, *spooky* is the word. Remember, whatever hides down in the abyss during the day comes up at night to feed, so keep your dive light and/or camera ready.

Nearest point of departure:	Freeport
Winter/summer water temperature:	65°F/84°F
Typical depth range:	52–80 feet
Typical water conditions:	Highly variable
Visibility:	To 125 feet
Expertise required:	Intermediate

After an 8-hour boat ride, and perhaps months of anticipation, your first glimpse of these unique reefs may be deceptively disappointing. From just below the water surface they appear to be just an ordinary rocky bottom. But after descending 55 to 60 feet, the landscape turns into a wild array of spectacular coral heads measuring up to 10 feet across. Huge boulders of

The Flower Gardens, Texas' backyard Caribbean reef, are located 100 miles southeast of Galveston. The large corals and colorful encrusting sponges make these two reefs the state's premier offshore diving destination.

The spectacular scenery afforded by 100-foot visibility at these marine gardens astonishes first-time divers.

A curious rock beauty peers out of a secure coral recess.

mountainous star coral and brain coral covered by brilliantly colored sponges jut upwards, providing an urban-like setting for more than 500 species of fish, macro-invertebrates, and algae.

The East and West Flower Garden Banks lie atop salt domes 110 miles southeast of Galveston at the edge of the Texas-Louisiana outer continental shelf. Situated 12 miles apart in 400 feet of water, these reefs are the northernmost reef system on the North American continental shelf. The crest of the East Flower Garden Bank covers 400 acres and lies 52 feet from the surface. The West Flower Garden Bank grows up to 66 feet

The Spanish hogfish, a common inhabitant of the Flower Gardens, is most often seen in its juvenile form. It spends much of its time as a parasite cleaner for other fish.

The queen angelfish is one of the most colorful tropical fish of these reef communities.

from the surface and covers 100 acres at the crest. Their very existence has intrigued marine scientists because they lie at the fringe of normal, reef-building habitat, 500 miles from their closest coral neighbor near Tampico, Mexico.

For the thrill of a lifetime, watch for the magnificent Atlantic manta gliding in from the depths off the shelf. These gentle and curious creatures, which

A smooth trunkfish and stoplight parrotfish investigate the bottom for food.

Colonies of tiny coral polyps have lived and died at this site for 20,000 years, creating a delicate and complex ecosystem.

can span 20 feet across at the wingtips, seem to enjoy being touched or even ridden by divers. Even if the manta isn't there on the day you dive, there's enough excitement in watching reef denizens like the spiny lobster, feather worms, thorny oysters, groupers, amberjacks, great barracuda, red snapper, and a host of tropical fish. Of special interest at the West Flower Gardens, but not accessible by divers, is a small brine lake discovered at 220 feet in

On a night dive at the Flower Gardens, one may encounter the colorful spiny lobster.

The main attraction at the Flower Gardens is the Atlantic manta. Curious and gentle, these majestic creatures can be seen on most visits, and a lucky diver may be able to hitch a ride.

Graceful tentacles of the nocturnal tube anemone extend into the darkness to feed on passing zooplankton.

Visitors to the Flower Gardens are always astonished at the large brain corals and diverse fish life.

1976 by Texas A&M University oceanographer, Dr. Tom Bright, in the submersible *Diaphus*.

Sadly, you will also see the abandoned chains, overturned coral heads, and wide, deep gouges caused by anchoring. After a 10-year battle by marine scientists, divers, and public officials, the Flower Gardens are finally in the process of being designated as a National Marine Sanctuary under the Marine Sanctuary Program established in 1972. The Marine and Estuary Management Division of the National Oceanic and Atmospheric Administration (NOAA) has authority over the designation. Regulating oil and gas activities, anchoring, and vessel sizes will protect these reefs from additional damage.

Along the same lines, refrain from spearfishing at the Flower Gardens. Spears can become embedded in live coral heads, further damaging the reefs. *For additional information,* contact a coastal dive shop.

The Department of Oceanography at Texas A&M University is involved in an extensive environmental monitoring study sponsored by the Department of the Interior's Minerals Management Service. You may see metal rods extending out of both live and dead coral heads. *Do not disturb these marker rods.* They are in place to measure long-term changes in coral growth and conditions. If these rods are tampered with in any way, a wealth of information may be lost.

4

Other Sites

The following are less frequently dived locations. For the offshore sites, contact a local or coastal dive shop to reserve space on a dive boat (see page 77).

Queen angelfish abound in the Flower Gardens off Texas' coast. ▲

Many dive trips to the Gulf involve consecutive deep dives. A dive computer will help to ▶ *get as much bottom time as possible.*

Expertise required:	Intermediate to advanced
Depth range:	60–90 feet
Visibility:	To 100 feet
Access:	Boat

Three Hickey Rocks is a trio of three spectacular pinnacles in the Gulf of Mexico, 140 miles southeast of Freeport. Rising in 300 feet of water, the peaks are approximately 75 feet in diameter and crest at 55 to 75 feet. Encrusting fire coral completely covers one pinnacle, lobsters flourish on another, and the third has neither coral nor lobsters. The pinnacles are about 1/2 mile apart.

Although they are well camouflaged, rock lobsters can be found at several of the offshore reefs.

Coordinates:	26°51′N, 97°18′W
Expertise required:	Intermediate
Currents:	Variable, can be very strong
Visibility:	15–25 feet
Access:	Boat

Named because it is located in 46 feet ($7^1/2$ fathoms) of water, this reef is 2 miles off Padre Island, 46 miles south of the northern entrance to the Padre Island National Seashore. It runs in a NW-SE direction, is 300 yards long, and 60 yards wide. The area used to be a freshwater lake during the last ice age when sea level was 350 feet lower. The reef contains fossils of mastadons, mammoths, and bison. This is not a very accessible site and visibility is highly variable because of its proximity to land.

An Atlantic deer cowrie can grow to five inches and is a common inhabitant of offshore destinations.

Depth range:	70–100 feet
Expertise required:	Advanced
Visibility:	To 100 feet
Access:	Boat

Sometimes called "liberty reefs," these 8 surplus WWII Liberty Ships were sunk along the Gulf Coast in 1975 and 1976 to create artificial reefs. Their marine life is similar to that found at the *V.A. Fogg*, and the bow of one ship actually sits 20 feet from the bow of the *V.A. Fogg*. The ships were sunk in at least 100 feet of water to avoid the soft, muddy bottom near shore. Because of this depth, only more experienced divers should visit the ships.

A safety stop at ten feet is recommended whenever diving deep wreck dive locations.

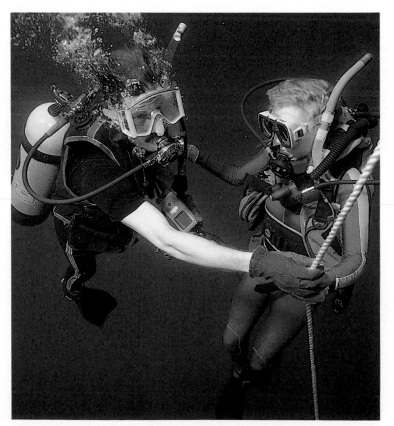

Closest air:	On site
Depth:	20–50 feet
Visibility:	5–15 feet

Squaw Creek lies halfway between Granbury and Glen Rose off Highway 144, 45 miles southwest of Ft. Worth. It was constructed 14 years ago by the Texas Utilities Commission as a cooling pond for a nuclear power plant being built at the site. The plant is due to become operational by the end of 1989. Squaw Creek Park is the only public access to the lake, and has facilities for fishing, swimming, and camping. Closest air is less than a mile away at Squaw Creek Divers (817) 573-8071, open only on weekends. The Park strictly regulates activities. Before diving here, call the dive shop and Texas Utilities at (817) 573-7053 for updates on diving conditions and regulations.

Divers take a surface interval at Squaw Creek.

5

Safety

This section discusses emergency procedures in case of a diving accident. We do not discuss the diagnosis or treatment of serious medical problems; refer to your first-aid manual or emergency diving accident manual for that information.

DAN

The Divers Alert Network (DAN), a membership association of individuals and organizations sharing a common interest in diving safety, operates a 24-hour national hotline—(919) 684-8111 (collect calls are accepted in an emergency). DAN does not directly provide medical care, however, the network does provide advice on early treatment, evacuation, and hyperbaric treatment of diving related injuries. Additionally, DAN provides diving safety information to members to help prevent accidents. Membership is $10 a year and offers:

- The DAN *Underwater Diving Accident Manual*, which describes symptoms of and first aid for the major diving-related injuries.
- Emergency room physician guidelines for drugs and I.V. fluids.
- A membership card listing diving-related symptoms on one side and DAN's emergency and non-emergency phone numbers on the other.
- One tank decal and three small equipment decals with DAN's logo and emergency number.
- A newsletter, *Alert Diver*, which describes diving medicine and safety information in layman's language and contains articles for professionals, case histories, and medical questions related to diving.

Special membership for dive stores, dive clubs, and corporations is also available. The DAN manual can be purchased for $4 from the Administrative Coordinator, National Diving Alert Network, Duke University Medical Center, Box 3823, Durham, NC 27710.

DAN divides the U.S. into 7 regions, each coordinated by a specialist in diving medicine who has access to the skilled hyperbaric chambers in his

Dive equipment should always be checked prior to taking your trip.

region. Non-emergency or information calls are connected to the DAN office and information number, (919) 684-2948. This number can be dialed directly, Monday–Friday, between 9 a.m. and 5 p.m. Eastern Standard time. Chamber status can change frequently, making this kind of information dangerous if obsolete at the time of an emergency. Instead, divers should contact DAN as soon as a diving emergency is suspected. All divers should have comprehensive medical insurance and check to make sure that hyperbaric treatment and air ambulance services are covered internationally.

Diving is a safe sport and there are very few accidents compared to the number of divers and number of dives made each year. But when the infrequent injury does occur, DAN is ready to help. DAN, originally 100% federally funded, is now largely supported by the diving public. Membership in DAN or purchase of DAN manuals or decals provides divers with useful safety information and provides DAN with necessary operating funds. Donations to DAN are tax deductible as DAN is a legal non-profit public service organization.

Emergency Services

In any emergency, your simplest and quickest contact for help is to dial 911. The following numbers can also be called for help:

Offshore Rescue:
 U.S. Coast Guard
 (409) 766-5620
 UHF radio: Channel 16

Hospitals/Recompression Facilities

**St. Elizabeth Hospital/
Hyperbaric Center**
2830 Calder
Beaumont, TX 77702
(409) 899-7067
Hyperbaric Oxygen Therapy Center
963 Ranchero Road
Kerrville, TX 78028
(512) 257-3013
**Southwest Methodist Hospital/
HBO Section**
4499 Medical Dr.
San Antonio, TX 78229
(512) 696-7293

**Memorial Medical Center/
Hyperbaric Unit**
2606 Hospital Blvd.
Corpus Christi, TX 78403
(512) 881-4372
St. David's Community Hospital
919 East 32nd Street
Austin, TX 78705
(512) 397-4145
Midland Memorial Hospital
2200 W. Illinois
Midland, TX 79701
(915) 685-1111
Maxfield Radiological Center
8215 Westchester, Suite 135
Dallas, TX 75225
(214) 987-1222
**Marine Biomedical
Institute/HBO**
200 University Blvd., Suite 600
Galveston, TX 77550
(409) 761-1307
**Memorial City Medical
Center/Hyperbaric Medicine**
920 Frostwood
Houston, TX 77024
(713) 932-4370

Appendix 1: Dive Shops*

This information is included as a service to the reader. The authors have made every effort to make this list accurate at the time the book was printed. This list does not constitute an endorsement of these operators and dive shops. If operators/owners wish to be considered for future reprints/editions, please contact Pisces Books, P.O. Box 2608, Houston, Texas 77252-2608.

Coastal Texas

Aquaventures Dive Shop
4099-B Calder
Beaumont, TX 77706
(409) 899-5331

See Sea Divers
4012 Weber
Corpus Christi, TX 78411
(512) 853-3483

Diver's Education & Equipment Place
4104 Seawall Blvd
Galveston, TX 77550
(409) 765-9746

The Dive Shop
2500 Padre Blvd
S. Padre Island, TX 78597
(512) 943-6635

Island Sea Sports, Inc.
736 Tarpon Street
Port Aransas, TX 78373
(512) 749-4167

Dolphin Divers
9501-B Nauarro
Victoria, TX 77904
(512) 576-6770

East Texas

Athen's Scuba Park
601 North Wofford
Athens, TX 75751
(903) 675-5762

Gulf Safari, Inc.
716 North 288
Clute, TX 77531
(409) 265-8401

Conroe Scuba & Ski, Inc.
812 West Dallas
Conroe, TX 77301
(409) 539-1414

Golden Mermaid
2420 North Frazier
Conroe, TX 77301
(409) 539-3483

All American Divers
7543 Westheimer
Houston, TX 77063
(713) 977-0028

Divetech, Inc.
8713-A Katy Freeway
Houston, TX 77024
(713) 973-2946

Kenlee's Scuba West
5539 Richmond
Houston, TX 77056
(713) 784-1173

ProScuba
9717 Westheimer
Houston, TX 77042
(713) 783-3483

Sea Sports Scuba
10971 Northwest Freeway
Houston, TX 77092
(713) 688-7777

Southwest Scuba & Travel, Inc.
11640 Southwest Freeway
Houston, TX 77031
(713) 498-3483

Texas Scuba
5414 Katy Freeway
Houston, TX 77007
(713) 880-1287

Universal Scuba Distributors
14230 Westheimer
Houston, TX 77077
(713) 493-0344

W.W. Diving Co.
1307 First Street
Humble, TX 77338
(713) 540-1616; 446-8861

Scubasport
121 West Pipeline Road
Hurst, TX 76053
(817) 282-4626

Scubatec
406 South Medford
Lufkin, TX 75901
(409) 637-1797

Diver's Depot
P.O. Box 632687
Nacogdoches, TX 75963-2687
(409) 564-3483

Adventure Quest Scuba
17611 Kuykendahl
Spring, Texas
(713) 320-0001

Scuba Center
3320 Troup Highway, Suite 130

Tyler, TX 75701
(903) 595-2703

Discover Scuba
15106 Highway 3
Webster, TX 77598
(713) 480-8530

Divers Paradise, Inc.
20801 Gulf Freeway, Suite 10
Webster, TX 77598
(713) 332-9982

Sport Divers of Houston, Inc.
125 West Bay Area Blvd
Webster, TX 77598-4111
(713) 338-1611

Central Texas

A.K.A. Divers
2150 North Collins
Arlington, TX 76011
(817) 275-2181

Arlington Scuba Center
2414 West Park Row Drive
Arlington, TX 76013
(817) 265-6712

Austin Scuba Center
1004-B Romeria Drive
Austin, TX 78757
(512) 452-2216

Scubaland Adventures
10805 North Lamar
Austin, TX 78753
(512) 339-0733

Scuba Point Travis
11401 RR 2222
Austin, TX 78730
(512) 258-6646

Tom's Dive & Ski, Inc.
5909 Burnet Lane
Austin, TX 78757
(512) 451-3425

Totally Scuba
603 North I35
Belton, TX 76513
(817) 939-1458

Adventures Beneath The Sea
1015 West College
Carrollton, TX 75006
(214) 484-3483

For Divers Only
1235 South Josey #540
Carrollton, TX 75006
(214) 317-2822

The Scuba Connection
205 North Highway 67
Cedar Hill, TX 75104
(214) 291-2782

Aqua Adventures Greenville, Inc.
6846 Greenville Avenue, Suite 100
Dallas, TX 75231
(214) 696-6090

Plaeco Ski & Scuba World
227 Webb Chapel Village
Dallas, TX 75229
(214) 241-7547

Sand & Sea Scuba
9410 Walnut Street, Suite 112
Dallas, TX 75243
(214) 690-3483

Scuba West Aquatic Center
2552 Joe Field Road
Dallas, TX 75229
(214) 247-4577

Divers Isle
203 North Hampton Road
DeSoto, TX 75115
(214) 230-1481

Island Divers Inc.
1731 West University Drive
Denton, TX 76201
(817) 566-1537

Cuda Dive Shop
7410 Grapevine Highway, Suite E
Ft Worth, TX 76180
(817) 284-0451

Lone Star Scuba
2815 Altamere Drive
Ft. Worth, TX 76116
(817) 377-3483

Scubasphere, Inc.
6703 Camp Bowie
Ft Worth, TX 76116
(817) 731-1461

Aqua Adventures, Inc.
5418 Broadway Blvd.
Garland, TX 75043
(214) 240-8000

Outdoor Adventures
1122 Highway 4 South
Granbury, TX 76049
(817) 573-3426

Tucker's Dive Shop
2025 East Main Street
Grand Prairie, TX 75050
(214) 264-7305

Gator's Scuba Mart
2211 Cheyenne
Irving, TX 75062
(214) 255-9522

Pelican Pier Scuba
210 North Ft Hood Street
Killeen, TX 76541
(817) 554-3483

Aqua Sports
1108 Dobie Drive, Suite 103
Plano, TX 75074
(214) 424-6563

Ocean's Window
2301 North Central Expressway #140
Plano, TX 75075
(214) 423-3483

Bat's Scuba Fun Center
1147 Harry Wurzbach
San Antonio, TX 78209
(512) 829-1699

Dive World
8507 North McCullough
San Antonio, TX 78216
(512) 340-3721

Trident Diving Equipment
2110 West Avenue
San Antonio, TX 78201
(512) 734-7442

Tropical Divers
2250 Thousand Oaks, Suite 212
San Antonio, TX 78232
(512) 490-3483

Scuba Plus
1404 West Adams
Temple, TX 76501
(817) 773-4220

Duggan Diving
928 Coronado Blvd.
Universal City, TX 78148
(512) 658-7495

Ski-N-Sea
6001 West Waco Drive #614
Waco, TX 76710
(817) 776-3388

West Texas

School of Scuba
942 Walnut Street
Abilene, TX 79601
(915) 673-2949

Underwater Connection
4103 N. First
Abilene, TX 79603
(915) 677-0337

Scuba Sportz
2618 Wolflin Village
Amarillo, TX 79109
(806) 355-3443

Scuba Training Center
2201 South Western #103

P.O. Box 51208
Amarillo, TX 79159-1208
(806) 358-0727

Del Norte Diving
1041 Humble
El Paso, TX 79915
(915) 778-6337

Inner Space Divers of El Paso
3737 North Mesa, Suite J
El Paso, TX 79902
(915) 532-4107

The Best Little Dive Shop In Texas
3813-50th Street
Lubbock, TX 79413
(806) 792-3483

Falcon Marine, Inc.
1920 North Loop 250 West
Midland, TX 79707
(915) 697-3261

Stovall's Scuba Center
3325 West Wadley Avenue, #A-2
Midland, TX 79707-5750
(915) 699-5959

Scuba Connection
6231 W. 26th St.
Odessa, TX 79763
(915) 381-1261

Sports Unlimited
127 W. Nopal
Uvalde, TX 78801
(512) 278-2327

Appendix 2: Equipment Checklist

Diving Equipment

_____ tank
_____ backpack
_____ regulator
_____ mask
_____ fins
_____ snorkel
_____ wetsuit
_____ boots
_____ gloves
_____ weight belt
_____ pressure gauge
_____ depth gauge

_____ dive computer
_____ B. C.
_____ knife
_____ compass
_____ dive bag
_____ dive light
_____ batteries or charger
_____ dive tables
_____ log book
_____ watch
_____ bottom timer
_____ dive flag

_____ "glow sticks"
_____ odds and ends kit
_____ "O rings"
_____ protective clothing
_____ nylon line
_____ flag and float
_____ slate
_____ buoy
_____ lift bag
_____ fishing license

Personal Items

_____ shirts
_____ shorts
_____ underclothing
_____ shoes
_____ sandals
_____ sunscreen
_____ soap
_____ deodorant

_____ toothbrush
_____ hair dryer
_____ travel clock
_____ pants
_____ swimsuit
_____ socks
_____ hat
_____ sunglasses

_____ medications
_____ shampoo
_____ toothpaste
_____ hairbrush
_____ comb
_____ scissors

Photo Equipment

_____ camera bodies
_____ tripod
_____ light meter
_____ strobe arm
_____ chargers
_____ ports

_____ lens cleaner
_____ extra parts
_____ lenses
_____ strobes
_____ extension tubes
_____ batteries

_____ housings
_____ film
_____ tool kit
_____ silicone grease

Appendix 3:
Maps of Parks/Campgrounds
Near Dive Sites*

Balmorhea State Recreation Area

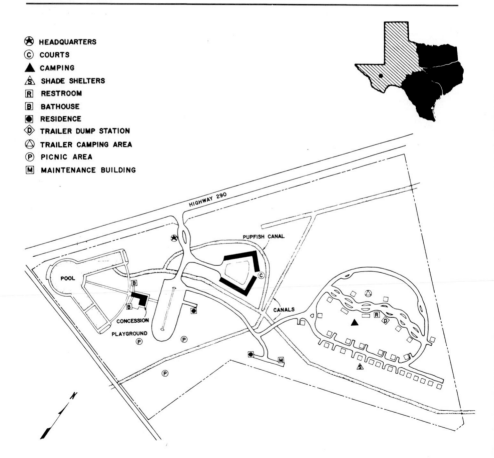

⊛ HEADQUARTERS
ⓒ COURTS
▲ CAMPING
Ⓢ SHADE SHELTERS
ℝ RESTROOM
Ⓑ BATHOUSE
◉ RESIDENCE
⬡ TRAILER DUMP STATION
△ TRAILER CAMPING AREA
Ⓟ PICNIC AREA
Ⓜ MAINTENANCE BUILDING

* From *Camper*'s *Guide to Texas Parks, Lakes, and Forests*, 3rd Edition by Mickey Little, Lone Star Books, Houston, Texas © 1990.

Lake Amistad

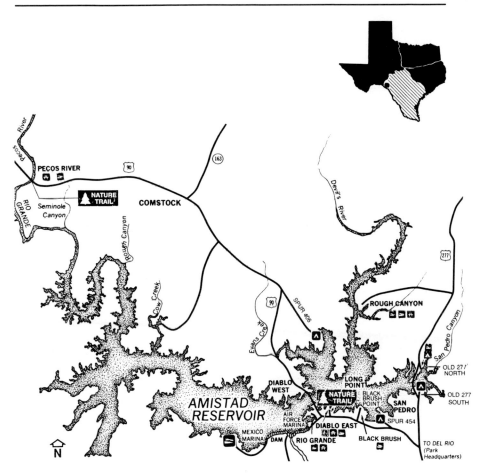

Picnic Area	
Hiking Trail	
Campground	
Boat ramps	
Swimming	

Garner State Park (Frio River)

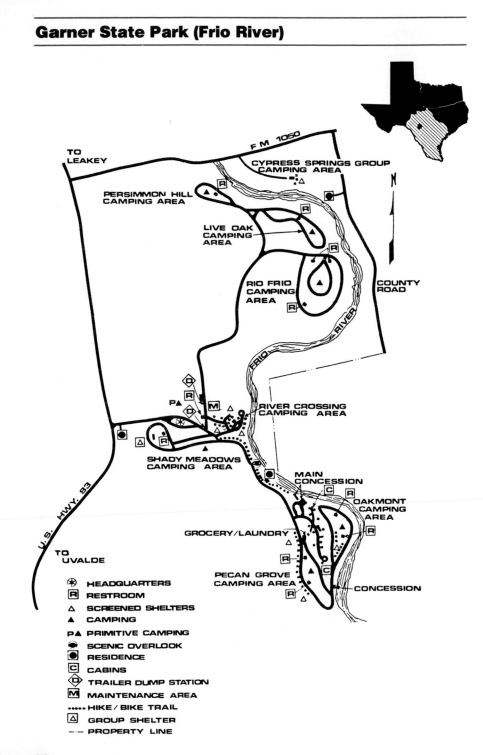

TO LEAKEY

F M 1050

CYPRESS SPRINGS GROUP CAMPING AREA

PERSIMMON HILL CAMPING AREA

LIVE OAK CAMPING AREA

RIO FRIO CAMPING AREA

COUNTY ROAD

FRIO RIVER

N

RIVER CROSSING CAMPING AREA

SHADY MEADOWS CAMPING AREA

MAIN CONCESSION

OAKMONT CAMPING AREA

GROCERY/LAUNDRY

PECAN GROVE CAMPING AREA

CONCESSION

U.S. HWY. 83

TO UVALDE

⊛ HEADQUARTERS
Ⓡ RESTROOM
△ SCREENED SHELTERS
▲ CAMPING
P▲ PRIMITIVE CAMPING
◉ SCENIC OVERLOOK
◙ RESIDENCE
ⓒ CABINS
◈ TRAILER DUMP STATION
Ⓜ MAINTENANCE AREA
····· HIKE / BIKE TRAIL
△ GROUP SHELTER
–·– PROPERTY LINE

Canyon Lake

Guadalupe River

POTTERS CREEK PARK

Canyon Lake Marina, Inc.

Cranes Mill Park Marina

CANYON PARK

CRANES MILL PARK

5th Army Retreat

CANYON LAKE

JACOBS CREEK PARK

LAKE CANYON YACHT CLUB

Randolph A.F.B. Recreation Area

NORTH PARK

CANYON CITY

GUADALUPE PARK

COMAL PARK

OVERLOOK PARK

HEADQUARTERS AREA

Guadalupe

STARTZVILLE

SATTLER

Scale of Miles

1   .5   0   1

Lake Travis

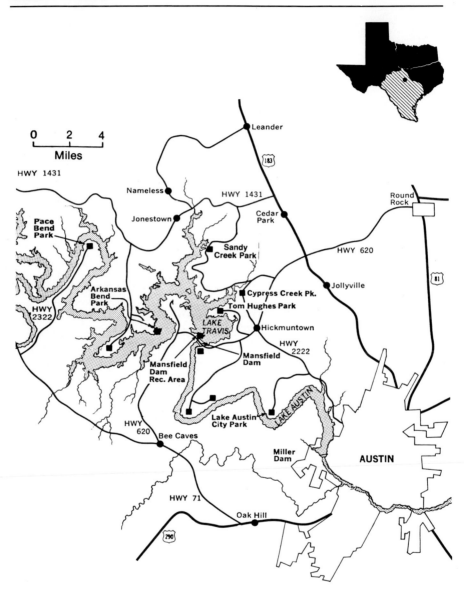

Possum Kingdom State Recreation Area

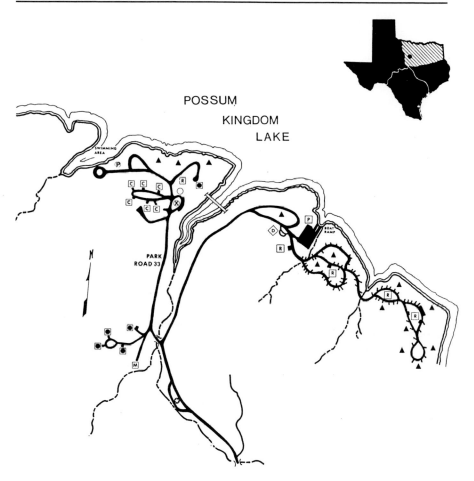

POSSUM

KINGDOM

LAKE

SWIMMING AREA

PARK ROAD 33

N

BOAT RAMP

LEGEND

✪ Headquarters	◈ Trailer Dump Station
◼ Residence	Ⓟ Parking Area
Ⓒ Cabin	Ⓜ Maintenance
Ⓡ Restroom	▲ Camping
ⓧ Playground	⊨ Fishing Pier
○ Concession	ℙ Picnicking

Huntsville State Park

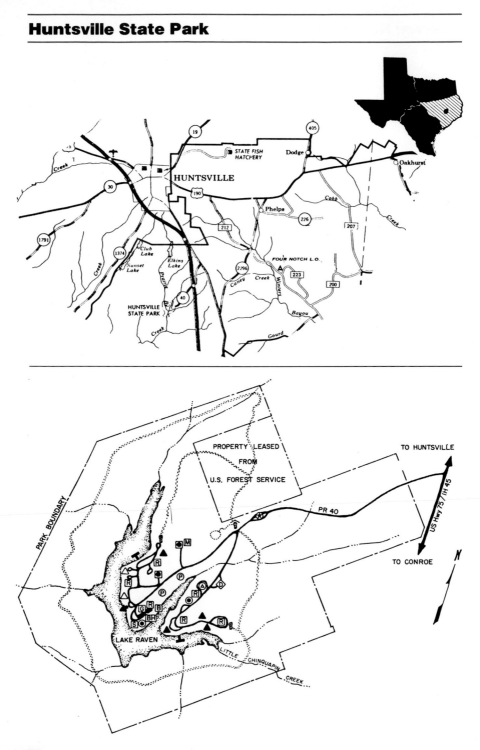

Toledo Bend Reservoir

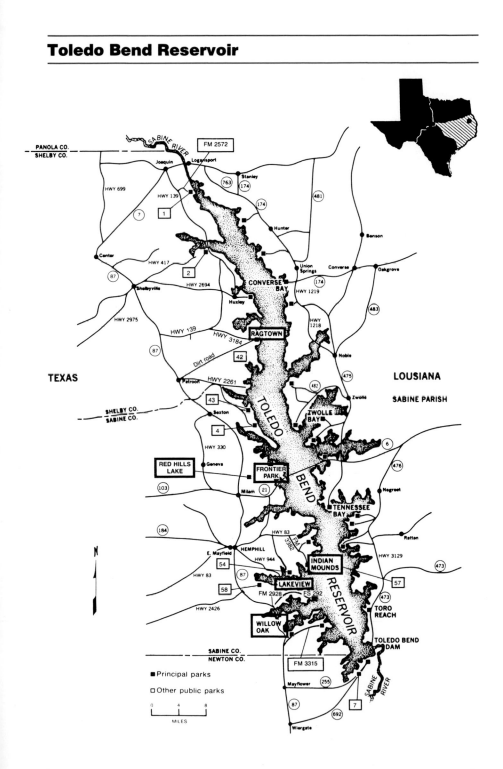

Index

Jetties, 41

Laguna Madre, 38
Lake Amistad, 12
Lake Possum Kingdom, 27
Lake Travis, 24
Liberty Ships, 70
Lobsters, 68
  spiny, 63

Manta rays, 62, 63
Map, 3
Marshall Ford Park, 25
Mexican tetras, 8, 19, 23
Monitoring study, 65
Mullet, 39

National Marine Sanctuary, 65
North Park, 17, 18

Octopus, 43
Oil rigs, 46
Offshore Diving, 44
  tips, 44
  hazards, 45
Other sites, 66
Overlook Park, 17, 18

Padre Island, 38, 69
Padre Island National Seashore, 38,
  69
Pecos mosquitofish, 8
Perch, 8, 15, 19, 35
  blue gill, 23, 27
  Rio Grande, 23
Port Aransas, 41
Possum Kingdom Recreation Area, 29
Prawn, freshwater, 19, 23

Ratings, definitions of, 2
Red snapper, 53, 63
Redfish, 39

Reefs, artificial, 46, 51, 70
  natural, 54, 59
Rio Grande River, 5, 12

Sabine River, 5, 34
Safety, 72
  DAN, 72
  emergency services, 74
San Pedro Cliffs, 13
San Marcos River, 5, 21
San Solomon Spring, 7
Sea urchins, 43
Sergeant majors, 53
Seven and One-Half Fathom Reef, 69
Sharks, 43, 57
Snail darter, 23
Soapfish, 49
Spadefish, 49, 53
Spearfishing
  game fish, 4
  offshore, 45
  oil rigs, 50
  regulations, 4
Sponges, 39, 43, 49, 53, 57, 61
Spring Lake, 21
Squaw Creek, 71
Starnes Island, 25
Stetson Bank, 54
Stingrays, 57

Texas Shark Fishing Contest, 43
Texas wild rice, 23
Thorny oyster, 63
Three Hickey Rocks, 68
Toadfish, 39
Toledo Bend, 34
Trout, speckled, 39
Turtles, 8, 23

V. A. Fogg, 51, 70

Whale sharks, 57
Windy Point, 25

Let these Pisces Diving and Snorkeling Guides show you the underwater wonders of—

Australia

Bahamas, Nassau, and
New Providence

Belize

Bonaire

California

Channel Islands

Cozumel

Dive into History:
U-Boats
U.S. Submarines
Warships

Fiji

Florida Keys and East Coast

Cayman Islands

Great Lakes

Great Reefs

Hawaii

Shipwreck Diving
New York & New Jersey
North Carolina
Southern California

Shooting Underwater Video

Snorkeling

Treasure Hunting with a Metal
Detector

Treasure of the Atocha

Turks & Caicos

Undersea Predators

The Underwater Dig—
An Introduction to
Marine Archaeology

Virgin Islands

Watching Fishes—
Understanding Coral Reef
Fish Behavior